UNDERSTANDING DISEASE AND WELLNESS

Kids' Guides to Why People Get Sick and How They Can Stay Well

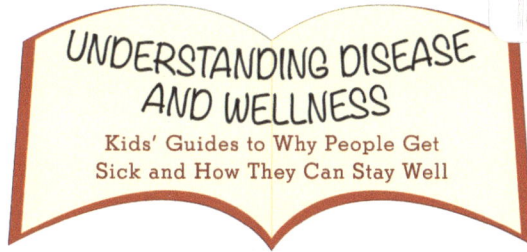

A KID'S GUIDE TO
CANCER

VILLAGE EARTH PRESS

Series List

UNDERSTANDING DISEASE
AND WELLNESS
Kids' Guides to Why People Get
Sick and How They Can Stay Well

A KID'S GUIDE TO CANCER

Rae Simons

Understanding Disease and Wellness:
Kids' Guides to Why People Get Sick and How They Can Stay Well
A KID'S GUIDE TO CANCER

Village Earth Press
Vestal, New York 13850
www.villageearthpress.com

First Printing
9 8 7 6 5 4 3 2 1

Series ISBN (paperback): 978-1-62524-445-1
ISBN (paperback): 978-1-62524-411-6
ebook ISBN: 978-1-62524-046-0
Library of Congress Control Number: 2013911239

Author: Simons, Rae

Note: This book is a revised and updated edition of *Cancer & Kids* (ISBN: 978-1-934970-14-0), published in 2009 by Alpha House Publishing.

Introduction

According to a recent study reported in the Virginia Henderson International Nursing Library, kids worry about getting sick. They worry about AIDS and cancer, about allergies and the "super-germs" that resist medication. They know about these ills—but they don't always understand what causes them or how they can be prevented.

Unfortunately, most 9- to 11-year-olds, the study found, get their information about diseases like AIDS from friends and television; only 20 percent of the children interviewed based their understanding of illness on facts they had learned at school. Too often, kids believe urban legends, schoolyard folktales, and exaggerated movie plots. Oftentimes, misinformation like this only makes their worries worse. The January 2008 *Child Health News* reported that 55 percent of all children between 9 and 13 "worry almost all the time" about illness.

This series, **Understanding Disease and Wellness**, offers readers clear information on various illnesses and conditions, as well as the immunizations that can prevent many diseases. The books dispel the myths with clearly presented facts and colorful, accurate illustrations. Better yet, these books will help kids understand not only illness—but also what they can do to stay as healthy as possible.

—*Dr. Elise Berlan*

Just the Facts

- There are many types of cancer. The one thing they all have in common is that they hurt the part of the cell that makes it split into two cells. This makes the cells spread through the body. It makes cells grow and grow, when they shouldn't.

- Cancer cells form tumors, which literally squish parts of the body, making people very sick. A tumor starts in one part of the body, but it can spread to other parts.

- Scientists around the world are studying the causes of cancer. Pollution, smoking, the sun, and even the parts of you passed along to you by your parents can all cause cancer.

- Doctors have several ways to find cancers, including blood tests, X-rays, and MRIs.

- Cancer is usually treated by cutting out the tumor and then giving the person special chemicals or radiation to keep the cancer from coming back.

- There are many people working for a cure for cancer around the world, including famous celebrities.

What Is Cancer?

Cancer is the name for a group of more than a hundred diseases. These different diseases all have something in common: cells in a part of the body begin to grow out of control. Untreated cancers can make people very sick and even die.

Normal body cells grow, divide, and die according to schedule. When you're young, your cells divide more quickly. Then the process slows down as you become an adult. After that, most of your cells divide only to replace worn-out or dying cells and to repair injuries.

Cancer cells, like the one shown here, start growing when the DNA in cells is damaged.

Words to Know

Inherit: get something that was passed down to you from your parents.

Environment: all the living and nonliving things that surround us.

DNA is what tells a cell what to do, including when to divide. Usually when DNA is damaged, either the cell dies or it repairs the DNA. That doesn't happen in cancer cells. People can *inherit* damaged DNA from their parents, but most often DNA is damaged by things in the *environment*. Chemicals, viruses, tobacco smoke, or too much sunlight can all damage cells.

ASK THE DOCTOR

My mother has lung cancer. Does that mean I'll get cancer, too?

Answer: No, it doesn't. Your mother may have cancer because she smoked or because of some other thing in her environment that doesn't affect you. If you have two close relatives with cancer, it's possible you too will have a genetic tendency to develop this disease. But even if you have inherited a "cancer gene," that doesn't mean you will definitely get cancer. It just means that if other conditions in the environment are right, your odds are higher for getting it than other people's are. Living a healthy lifestyle will be even more important.

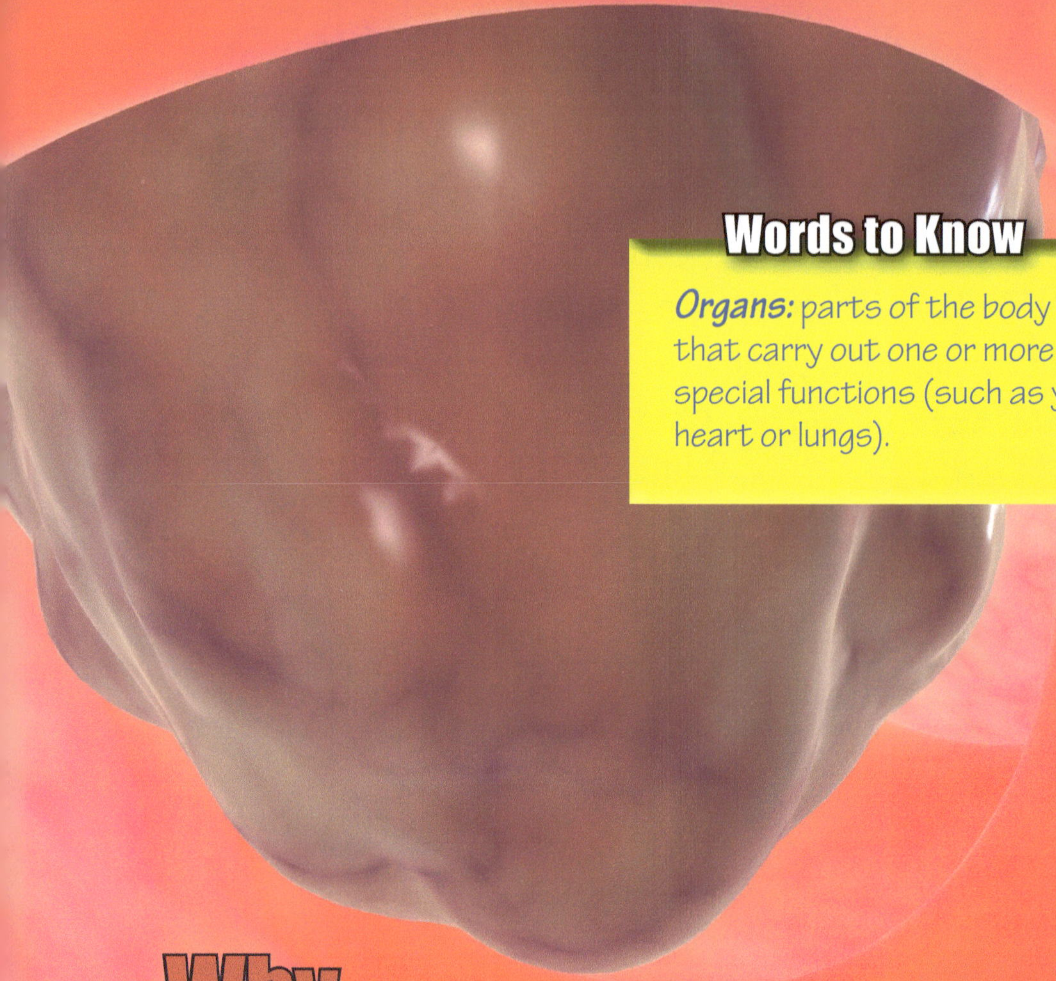

Words to Know

Organs: parts of the body that carry out one or more special functions (such as your heart or lungs).

Why Does Cancer Make People Sick?

Because cancer cells keep growing and dividing, they live longer than normal cells. They make more and more new cancer cells. These abnormal cells often form a tumor (a lump or mass) like the one shown above. These lumps can push on other body *organs*. The tumors can get in the way of organs doing their jobs. Eventually, organs will be damaged.

Cancer cells of all sorts often travel through the bloodstream or through the *lymph* system to other parts of the body. Then they grow in a new place and replace normal cells there. Some cancers, like leukemia, do not form tumors, because they are in a person's blood.

Words to Know

Lymph: a clear, watery fluid from body tissues that contains white blood cells and flows throughout the body.

11

Kinds of Cancer

Cancers that begin in different parts of the body can act very differently from each other. They grow at different rates. They respond to different treatments.

The cancer cell shown to the right is in the blood stream. That means it has broken off from the tumor where it started. Now it may end up growing in another part of the body.

Even when cancer has spread to a different part of the body, it is still named for the place in the body where it started. For example, breast cancer that has spread to the liver is called *metastatic* breast cancer, not liver cancer.

Some of the most common kinds of cancer are:

> leukemia
> lung cancer
> skin cancer
> colon cancer

Words to Know

Metastatic: having to do with cancer cells spreading through the body.

Did You Know?

Half of all men and one-third of all women will develop cancer during their lifetimes. Today, millions of people are living with cancer or have had cancer. The risk of getting most types of cancer can be made smaller, though, by lifestyle changes. Quitting smoking, not staying out in the sun, exercising, and eating a healthy diet are all ways to protect yourself from cancer. And the sooner a cancer is found and treated, the better the chances are for living for many years.

Leukemia

Leukemia is a kind of cancer that affects the white blood cells. These cells normally kill any germs that get in your blood. They help keep you healthy. When someone has leukemia, though, abnormal white blood cells are made in the bone marrow. These abnormal cells crowd the bone marrow and flood the bloodstream—but they cannot do the white blood cells' job of protecting the body against disease.

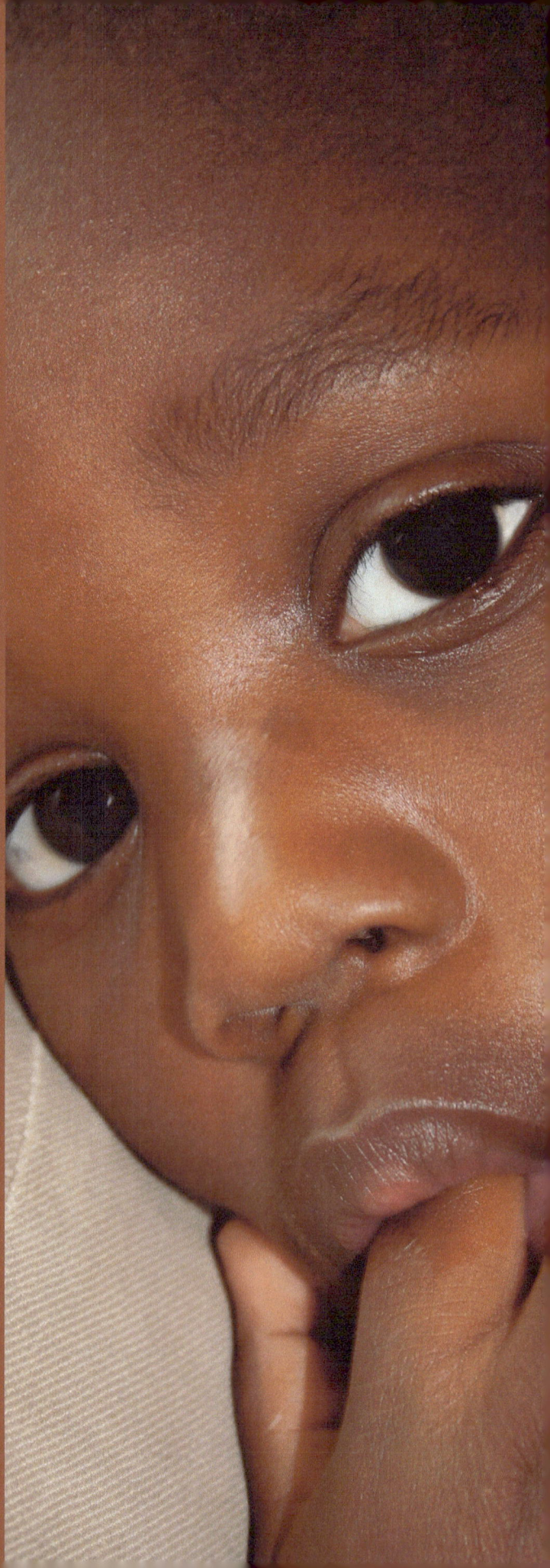

Anemia: a condition where there are fewer healthy red blood cells than normal. Since red blood cells carry the oxygen your body's cells need for energy, anemia can make you feel tired and weak.

As leukemia gets worse, it keeps the body from making other types of blood cells, including red blood cells. This causes *anemia* and bleeding problems. It also means the person is even more likely to catch other infections.

Leukemia is a kind of cancer that children get. Luckily, the chances for a cure are very good with leukemia. With treatment, most children with leukemia get better—and the leukemia never comes back!

Lung Cancer

Lung cancer is caused by abnormal cells growing in the lungs, usually in the cells lining tubes inside the lungs. This growth may eventually spread to the body parts around the lungs as well. It can also *metastasize* and spread through the body.

Lung cancer is the most common cause of cancer-related death in men. It's the second most common in women. Around the world, 1.3 million people die from it each year.

The most common symptoms of lung cancer are shortness of breath, coughing (including coughing up blood), and weight loss.

Words to Know

Metastasize: when cancer spreads to other parts of the body.

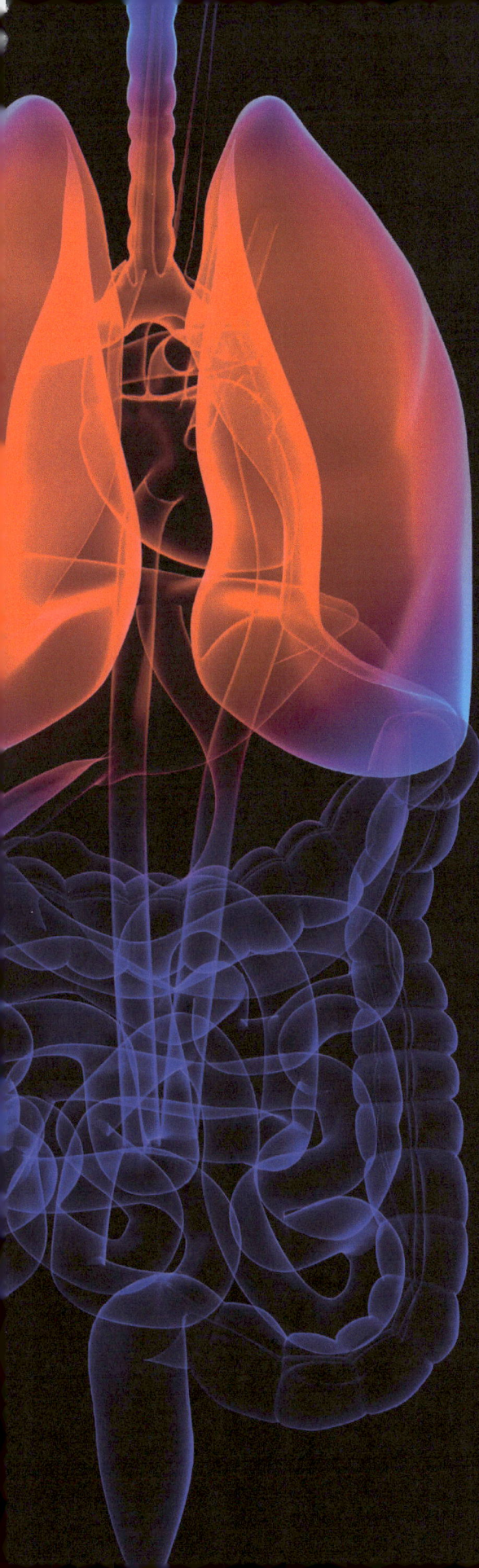

Mostly older people get lung cancer—and 90 percent of them are smokers. (In other words, if you have a group of ten people with lung cancer, nine of them would probably smoke.) Before the 1930s, lung cancer was very rare. As more people started smoking, more people got cancer. Among those people who smoke two or more packs of cigarettes per day, one in seven will die of lung cancer. Today, people in many countries are learning about the risks of smoking. Not as many people are getting lung cancer now, because fewer people are smoking.

Skin Cancer

Skin cancer is the abnormal growth of skin cells. It most often happens on skin *exposed* to the sun. Sometimes, though, it can also occur on skin that's not usually in the sun.

Most skin cancers can be prevented if you protect your skin from the sun's harmful rays. You should also pay attention to any changes to your skin, including any new spots (or spots that have changed in color or shape). Skin cancer can be treated successfully if you catch it early.

Words to Know

Exposed: placed where a condition or action can change something.

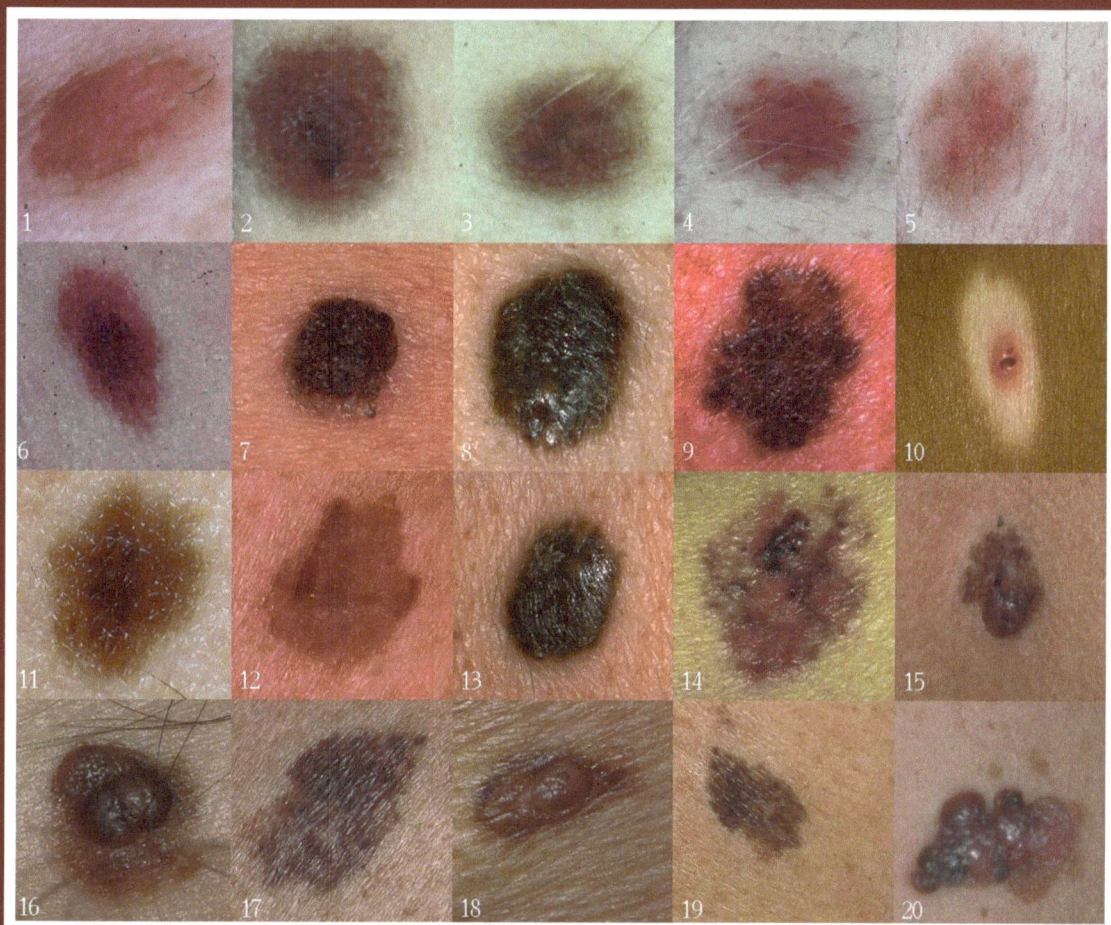

These are all examples of moles that are actually skin cancer. Tell a grownup (and go see your doctor) if you have a mole that gets bigger, changes shape, or changes color. Not all spots on your skin are cancer—but only a doctor can tell you for sure.

Colon Cancer

Did You Know?

Colon cancer is the third most common form of cancer and the second leading cause of cancer-related death in Europe and North America. Colon cancer causes 655,000 deaths worldwide each year.

A person with colon cancer will have cancerous tumors in the colon (like the one shown to the right). Your colon is the tube through which waste materials pass. Food goes from your stomach into your small intestine. After it's been digested, what's left is waste material. It goes through your colon and eventually into the toilet. Your colon is also sometimes called your large intestine.

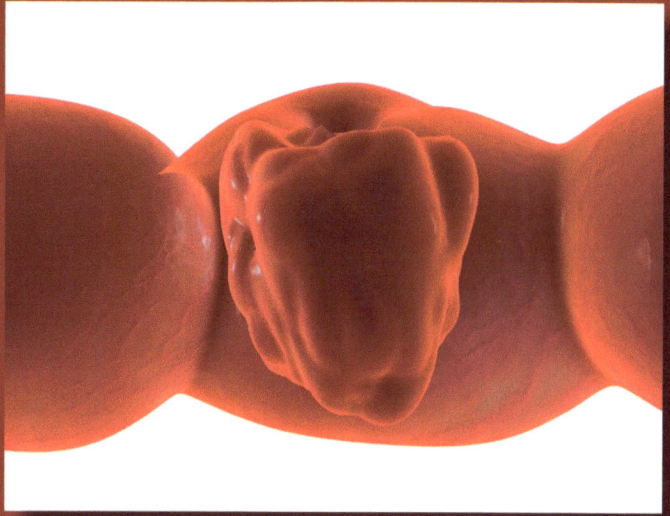

Most colon cancers start out as harmless *polyps* like the one shown to the left. These slowly change into cancer, but scientists are not sure why. Diet may play a role. Scientists believe that eating plenty of whole grains and other high-fiber foods may help keep your colon healthy.

See a doctor if you notice any change in your bowel movement habits.

Words to Know

Polyps: masses of tissue that develop on the inside of a hollow body organ.

Cancer and Genes

Scientists around the world are working hard to understand what causes cancer. They want to understand how a normal cell can turn into a cancer cell. Scientists have found that certain *genes* play a part in some cancers. Some people are born with a change in their genes (mutation) that makes them more likely to get cancer. When this happens, scientists say the people have inherited cancer genes.

This mutation may then also be passed on to their children.

There are two types of genetic changes or mutations. One kind is passed down from generation to generation. The other kind happens during a person's lifetime and is not passed on to the next generation.

Inherited genes become a part of you at the moment of *conception*. All the cells of your body develop from one fertilized egg. So if that egg contains a cancer gene, all the cells in your body will have the gene that puts you at risk of getting cancer.

Words to Know

Genes: the parts of chromosomes (the spiral shape shown on the page to the left) that contain the directions for how new cells are formed.

Conception: the moment when an egg is fertilized with a sperm, meaning it can become a new person or animal.

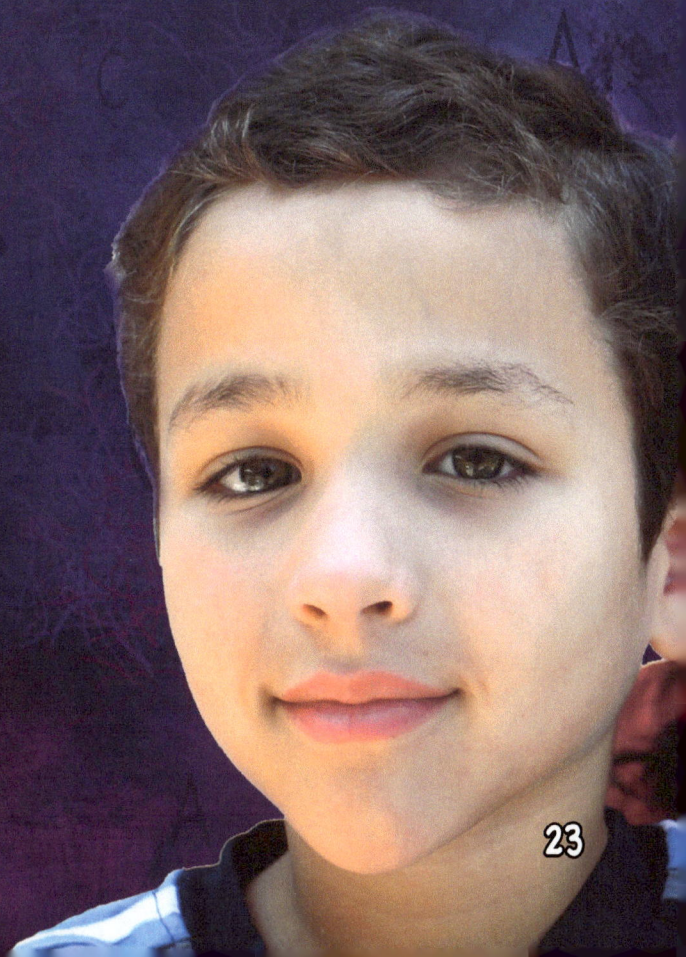

23

Cancer and the Environment

The good news is that most cancers are not inherited. As many as two-thirds of all cancer cases are linked to environmental causes. This means if we can change the environment, we can keep many of these cancers from happening.

Words to Know

Radiation: energy that comes from a source and travels through air, space, or some other material. Light, heat, and sound are types of radiation, but they don't cause cancer. The kind of radiation that causes cancer contains charged particles (ions) that can damage cells' genes.

Pollution increases our risk of getting cancer. Factories, cars, farms, and buildings put chemicals and *radiation* into our air, water, food, and homes. Then we take these chemicals into our bodies through our lungs, our mouths, and our skin. Once they're inside our bodies, they can trigger the cell changes that cause cancer.

Cancer and Lifestyle
Dangerous Sunshine

Most of us love sunshine. The sun's rays make us feel good. But sunshine isn't always good for us. In fact, it can cause cancer. The sun's *ultraviolet* (UV) radiation is the number-one cause of skin cancer. It triggers changes in skin cells' genes that can turn into cancer. And it doesn't matter how hot it is—being out in the sun too much during the winter puts you at the same risk as being in the sun in the summer.

The more times you've had a severe sunburn before you're eighteen, the more likely you are to have a serous form of skin cancer when you're older. Being out in the sun day after day, year after year, may give you a nice tan—but it also can cause a less serious form of skin cancer.

Words to Know

Ultraviolet: radiation with more energy than visible light.

ASK THE DOCTOR

My friends say that a safer way to get a suntan is to go to a tanning salon, where you won't even have to be in the sun to get a nice tan. Are they right?

Answer: No, they're not! Tanning beds also use ultraviolet rays to give you a tan—which means they can also cause skin cancer.

27

Did You Know?

Tobacco use causes more than five million deaths worldwide each year. If people keep smoking this much, tobacco use will cause more than eight million deaths a year by 2030. On average, smokers die thirteen to fourteen years earlier than nonsmokers.

The chemicals found in tobacco smoke also trigger changes in body cells that can lead to cancer. In fact, smoking damages nearly every organ in the human body. Scientists have linked smoking to at least fifteen different cancers. At least 30 percent of all deaths caused by cancer (that's about one-third) are caused by smoking. When it comes to lung cancer, the numbers are even worse: smoking causes 90 percent of all lung cancers.

So if you don't want to get lung cancer, there's something doctors know will help: don't smoke! And if you do smoke, quit! Smoking is one danger you can choose to avoid.

ASK THE DOCTOR

My dad smokes all the time. How dangerous is it that I breathe his smoke?

Answer: It's pretty dangerous. You need to ask your father not to smoke around you—and if he won't listen to you, open the window whenever you can, and leave the house until it's aired out. Let your father know that scientists have discovered that people who live with secondhand smoke all the time are very likely to develop lung cancer and other smoking-related cancers.

Diagnosing Cancer
Symptoms

Even thinking about cancer can make people feel scared. So some people don't like to think about cancer's warning signs. They'd rather just not think about anything to do with cancer!

But since so many cancers respond well to early treatment, if you have cancer, you need to find out as soon as possible. The sooner you know, the sooner you can begin treatment.

So keep an eye open for the seven symptoms listed on the next page. It's not a scary thing. It's a way to stay safe! It can save your life!

ASK THE DOCTOR

We just found out that my grandmother has breast cancer. Does that mean she's going to die?

Answer: No, it doesn't. Most women who get treatment for their cancer will live at least another five years. Many women will recover completely. It all depends on what kind of cancer your grandmother has and how soon it was found. Her doctor will be able to answer your questions so you know better what to expect.

The 7 Warning Signs of Cancer

1. Unusual bleeding or *discharge* from any part of your body.

2. A sore that doesn't heal.

3. A change in your bathroom habits.

4. A lump in your flesh.

5. A cough that doesn't go away.

6. A change in the shape or color of a mole.

7. Difficulty swallowing.

If you have any of these symptoms, tell a grownup—and make sure you see a doctor right away.

Words to Know

Discharge: flow of fluid from a part of the body.

Blood Tests

Blood tests alone usually can't tell a doctor if you have cancer. But they can give your doctor clues about what's going on inside your body. A nurse or *technician* will take a little blood from your arm and then do various tests on it in a *lab*.

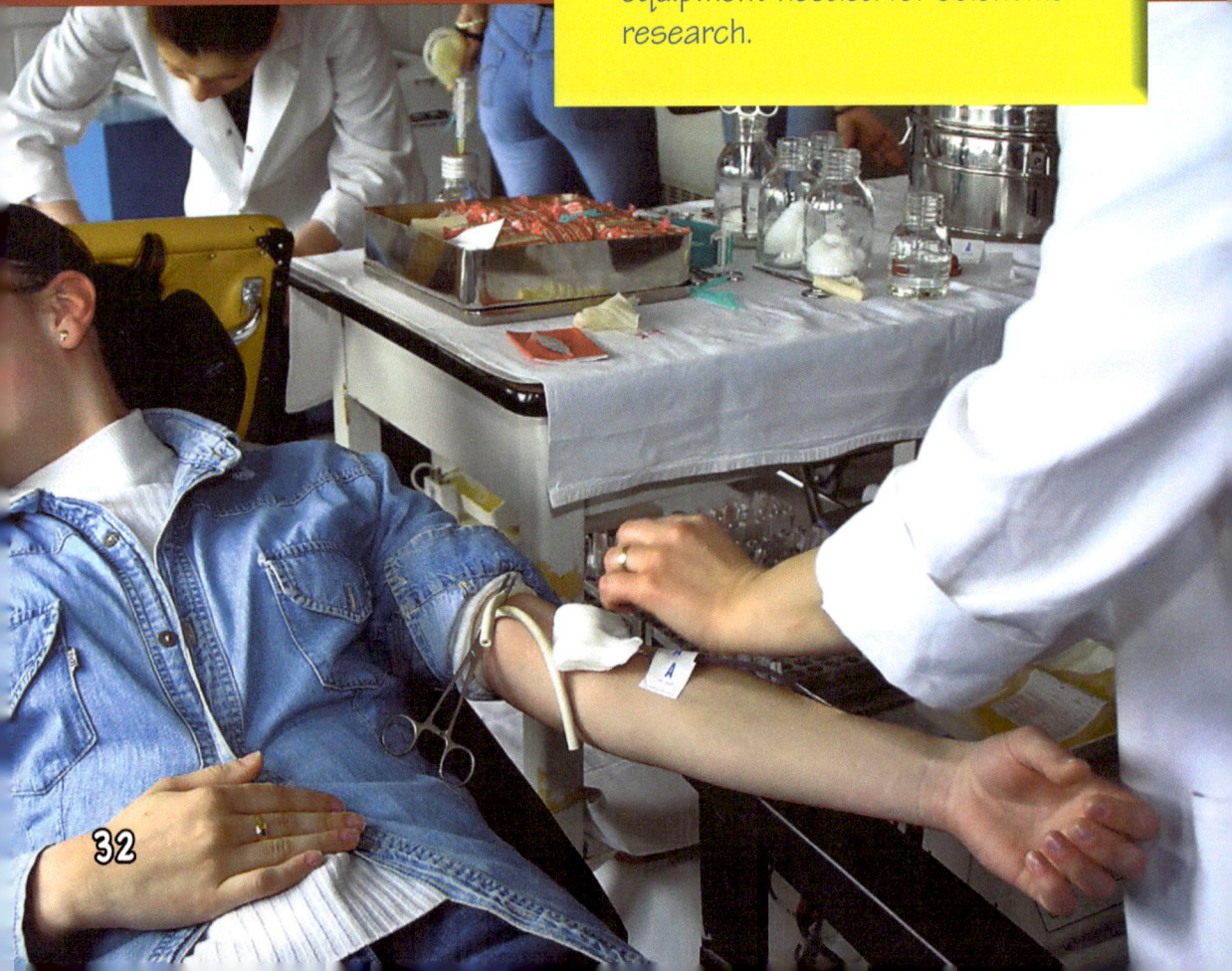

If the doctor finds cancer cells, too many or too few cells of a certain type, or abnormal types of cells, she may want you to have more tests.

For most forms of cancer, a biopsy is usually necessary before the doctor can know for sure. This means the doctor will cut out a little bit of cells. Sometimes the doctor will order other tests that allow her to "look inside" your body and see if anything is there that shouldn't be.

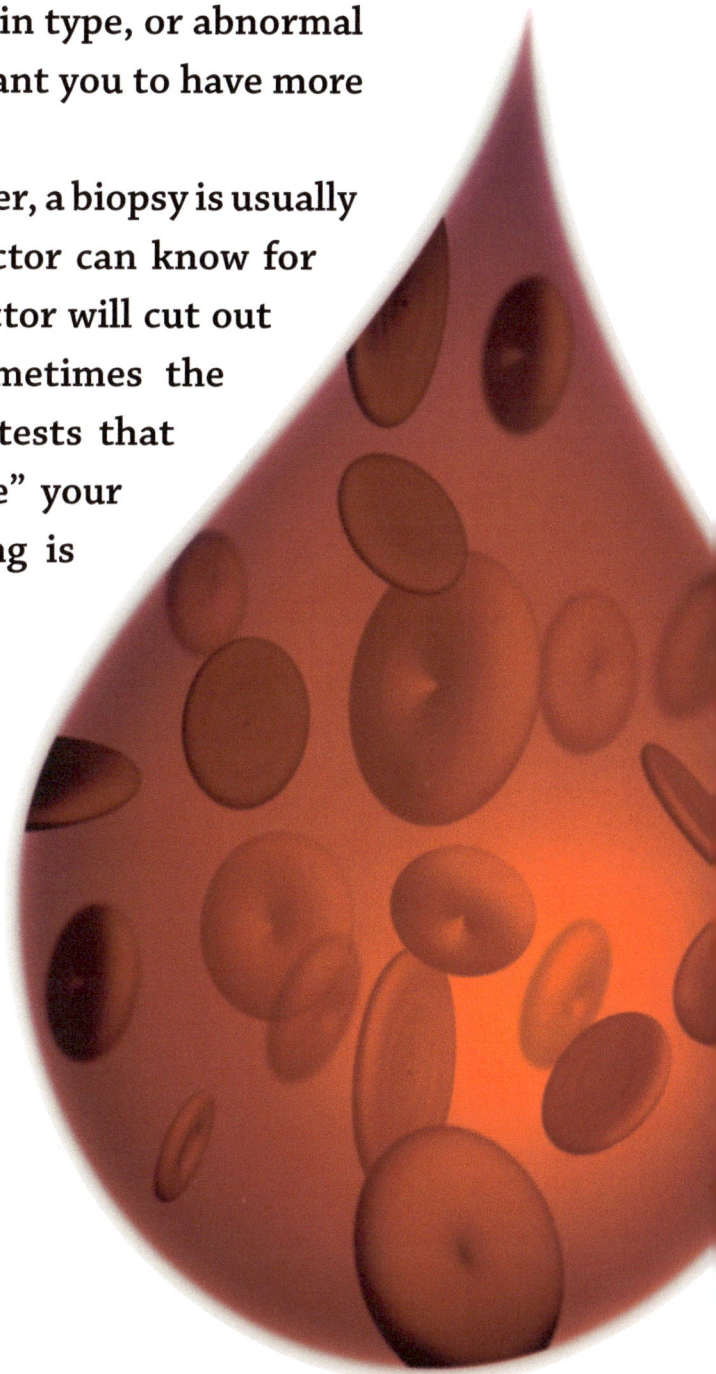

X-Rays

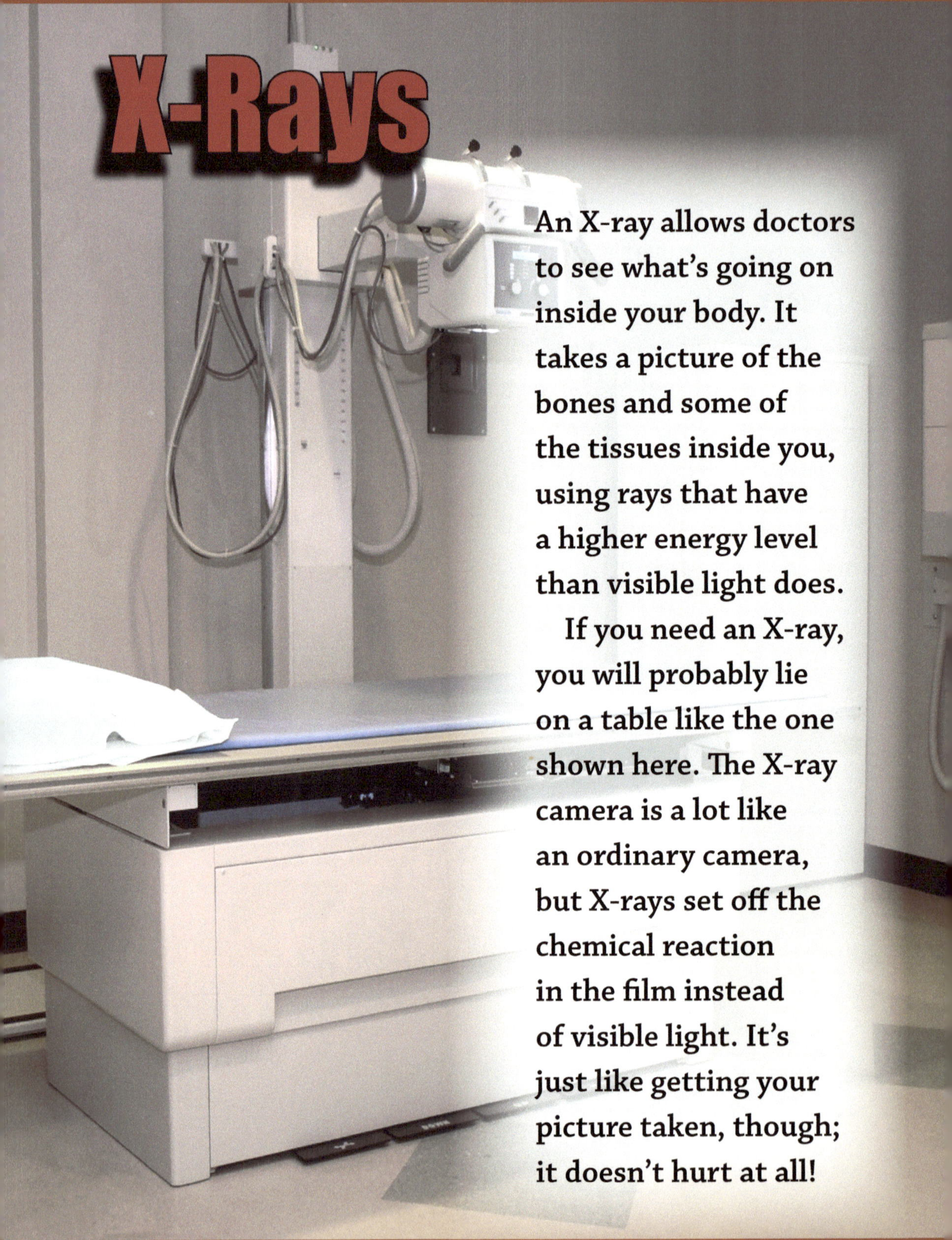

An X-ray allows doctors to see what's going on inside your body. It takes a picture of the bones and some of the tissues inside you, using rays that have a higher energy level than visible light does.

If you need an X-ray, you will probably lie on a table like the one shown here. The X-ray camera is a lot like an ordinary camera, but X-rays set off the chemical reaction in the film instead of visible light. It's just like getting your picture taken, though; it doesn't hurt at all!

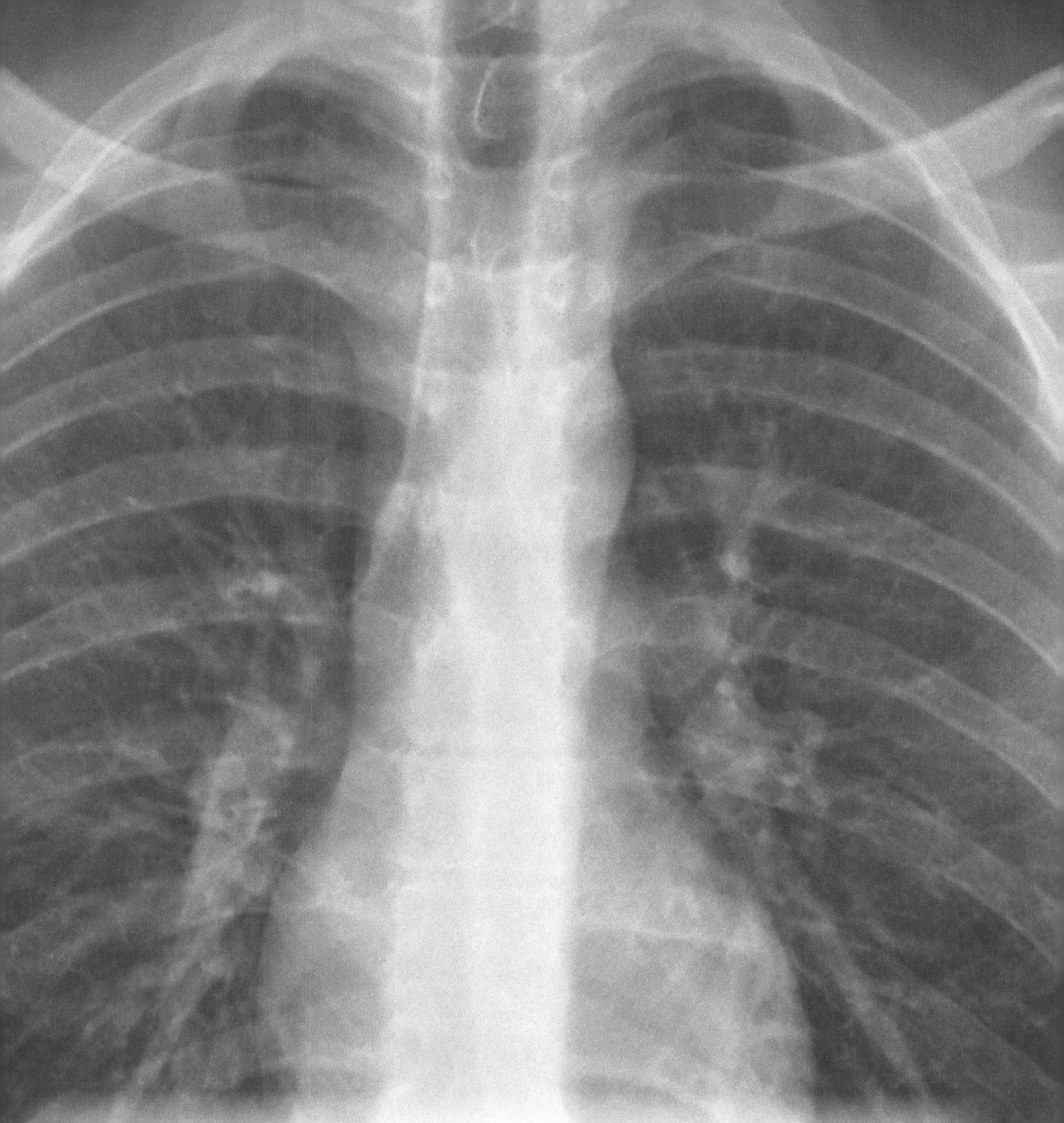

Doctors usually keep the film image as a negative. That means the areas that are exposed to more light look darker, and the areas that are exposed to less light look lighter. Hard material, such as bone, appears white, and softer material—such as a tumor—appears black or gray.

CAT Scans and MRIs

CAT scans use a special type of X-ray. The patient lies down on a couch that slides into a large circle-shaped opening. The X-ray tube circles around the patient. A computer collects the results. These results are turned into images that look like a "slice" of the person.

Did You Know?

Patients who have any metal inside their bodies (such as artificial joints, pacemakers, bullet fragments, or insulin pumps) should not have MRIs. The magnet could move the metal.

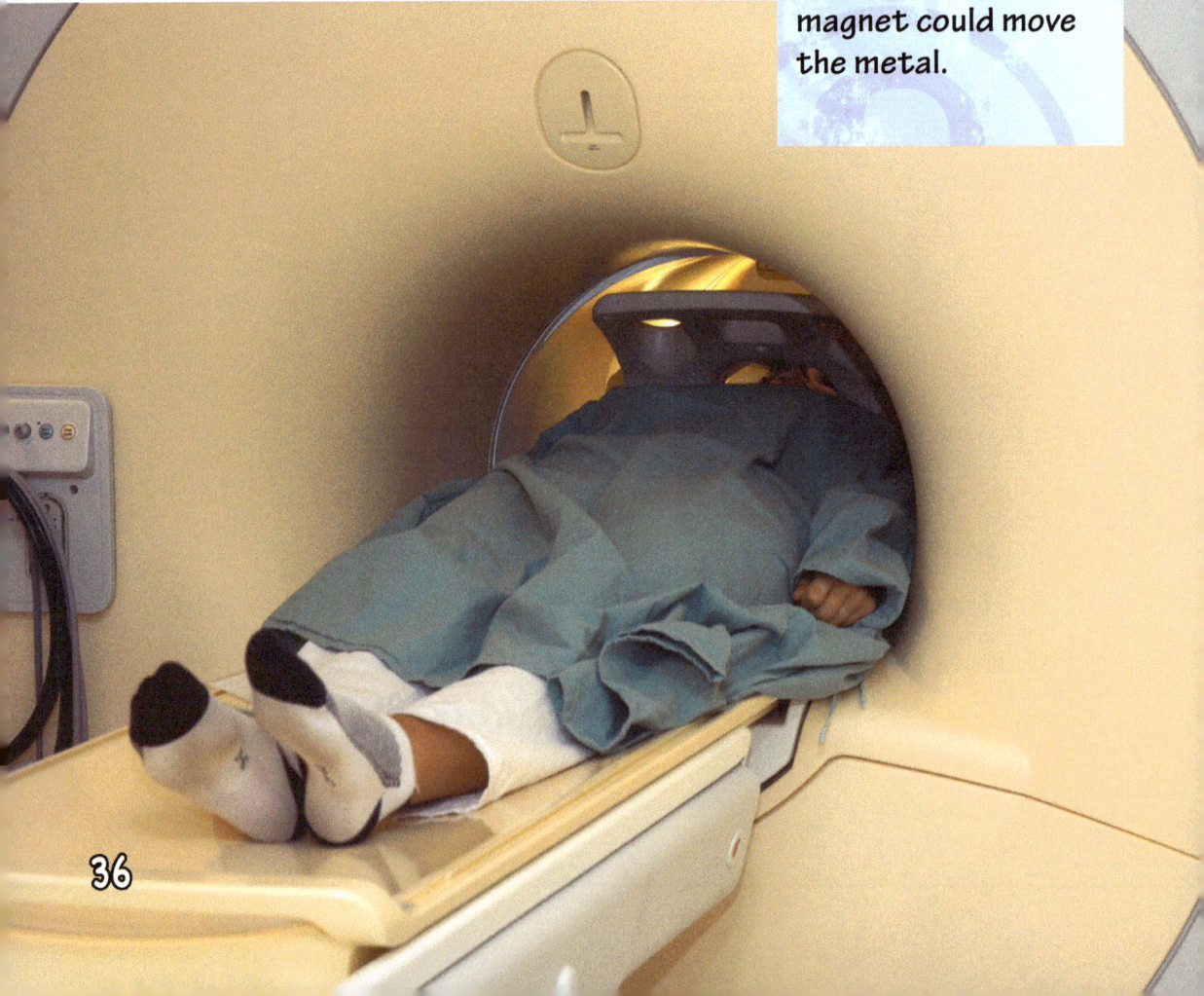

Tissues: a collection of body cells all working together to do the same job.

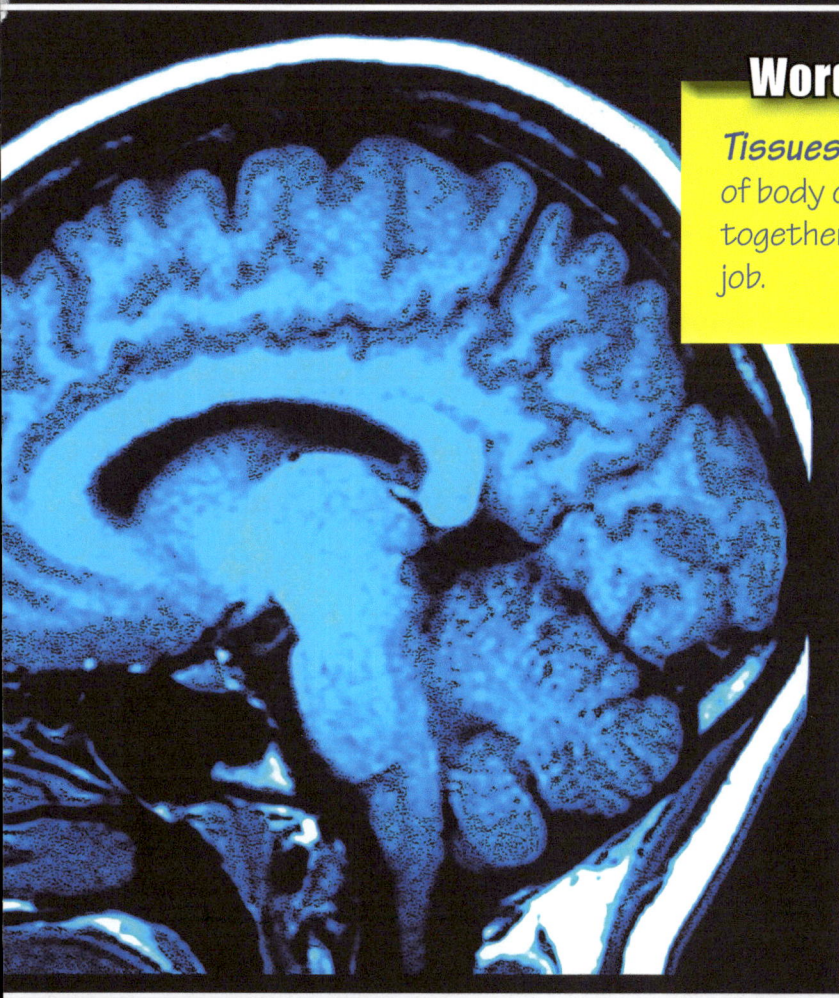

If you have an MRI, you will go inside a very long cylinder. You will be asked to stay perfectly still for about thirty minutes. The machine will make a lot of noise.

The cylinder you lie in is actually a very large magnet. Radio waves are sent through your body. Then a computer collects the signals and turns them into images. These images look like the ones that come from a CAT scan, but they show more details in soft *tissues*. This means they are useful for finding tumors and other abnormal masses.

The only way to know for sure if a tumor is cancer, though, is to cut out a little piece during surgery and test it.

Cancer Treatment

If you find out that you or someone you love has cancer, it's normal to feel scared and sad. But scientists and doctors have found many ways to treat cancer.

Getting cancer doesn't have to mean you're going to die! It probably will mean, though, that you spend some time in a hospital. You may not have to sleep there, but you will probably have to visit often to get the treatments you need.

If you have cancer, your body's *immune system* will be working hard to destroy the invaders in your body—the cancer cells that don't belong there. Cancer treatments help your body do its job better.

There are three main kinds of cancer treatment:

- surgery
- radiation treatment
- chemotherapy

Your doctor will help you decide which is best.

Words to Know

Immune system: the group of body parts that defends your body against diseases and infections.

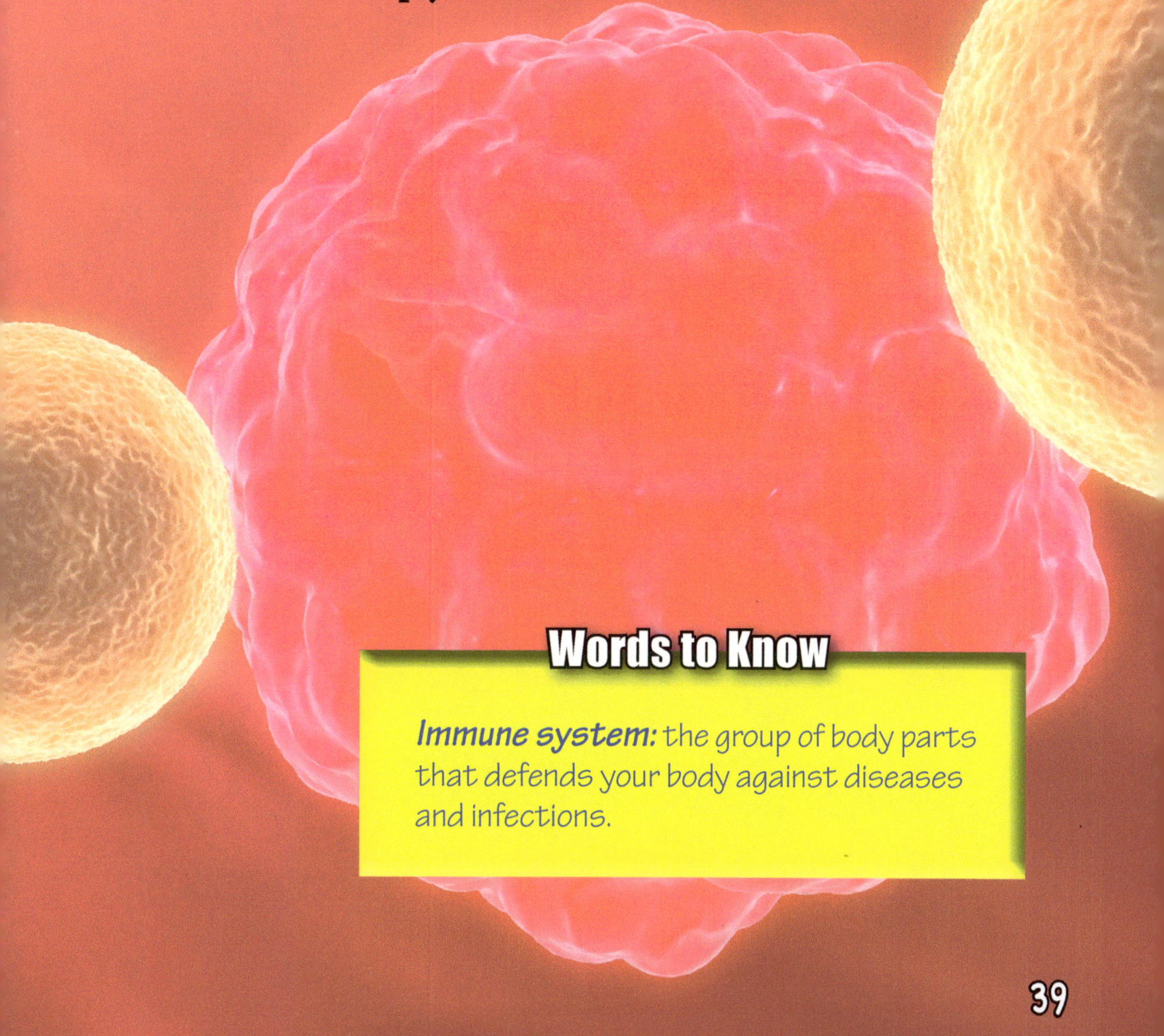

Oncologists

Diagnose: figure out the cause or disease that's causing symptoms.

Physiotherapy: treatment to help people move their joints and muscles without pain.

Oncologists are special cancer doctors. Oncology is the branch of medicine that studies tumors (cancer). Oncologists try to understand why cancer grows the way it does. They try to find better ways to *diagnose* and treat it. They also look for ways to prevent it. Oncologists often manage cancer patients' complete care. This means they work with other doctors who also treat these patients. Oncologists may also arrange for *physiotherapy* and counseling.

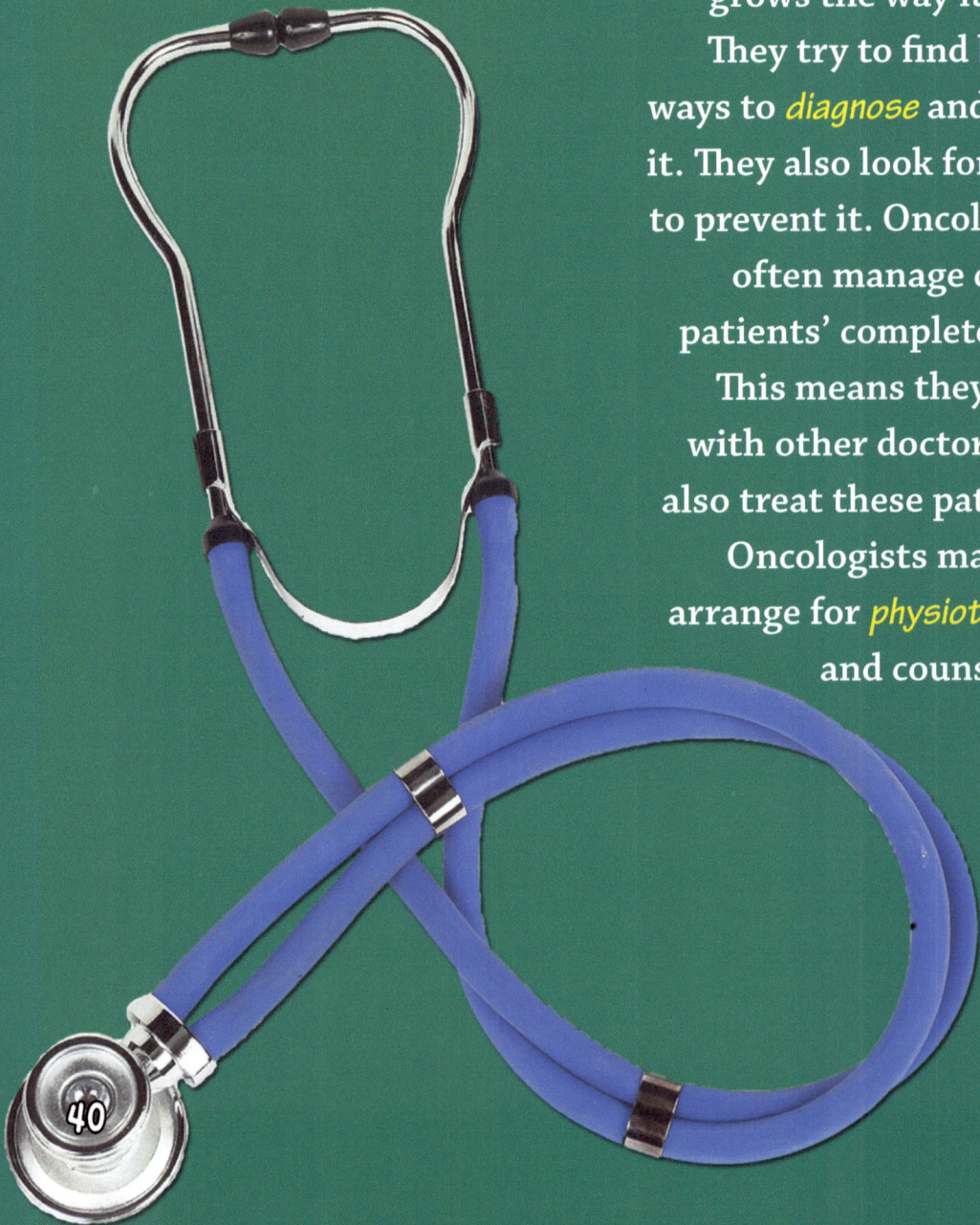

40

Oncologists are the doctors who diagnose whether someone has cancer. They're the doctors who oversee cancer treatment. After treatment is over, they follow up with cancer patients, checking them regularly to make sure they stay healthy.

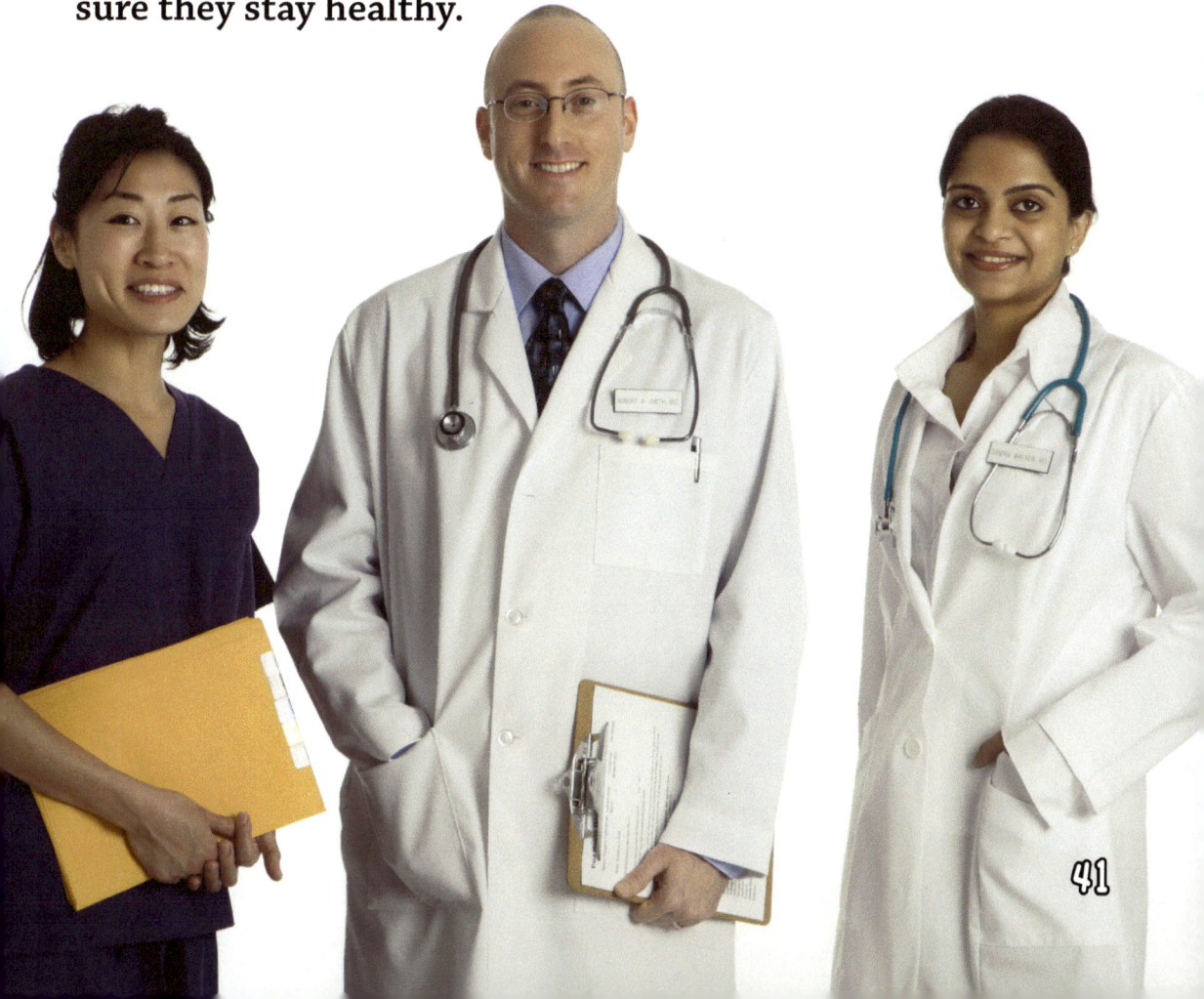

41

Words to Know

Anesthesiologist: a doctor whose job is to give patients anesthesia, the medicine that makes them go to sleep during surgery.

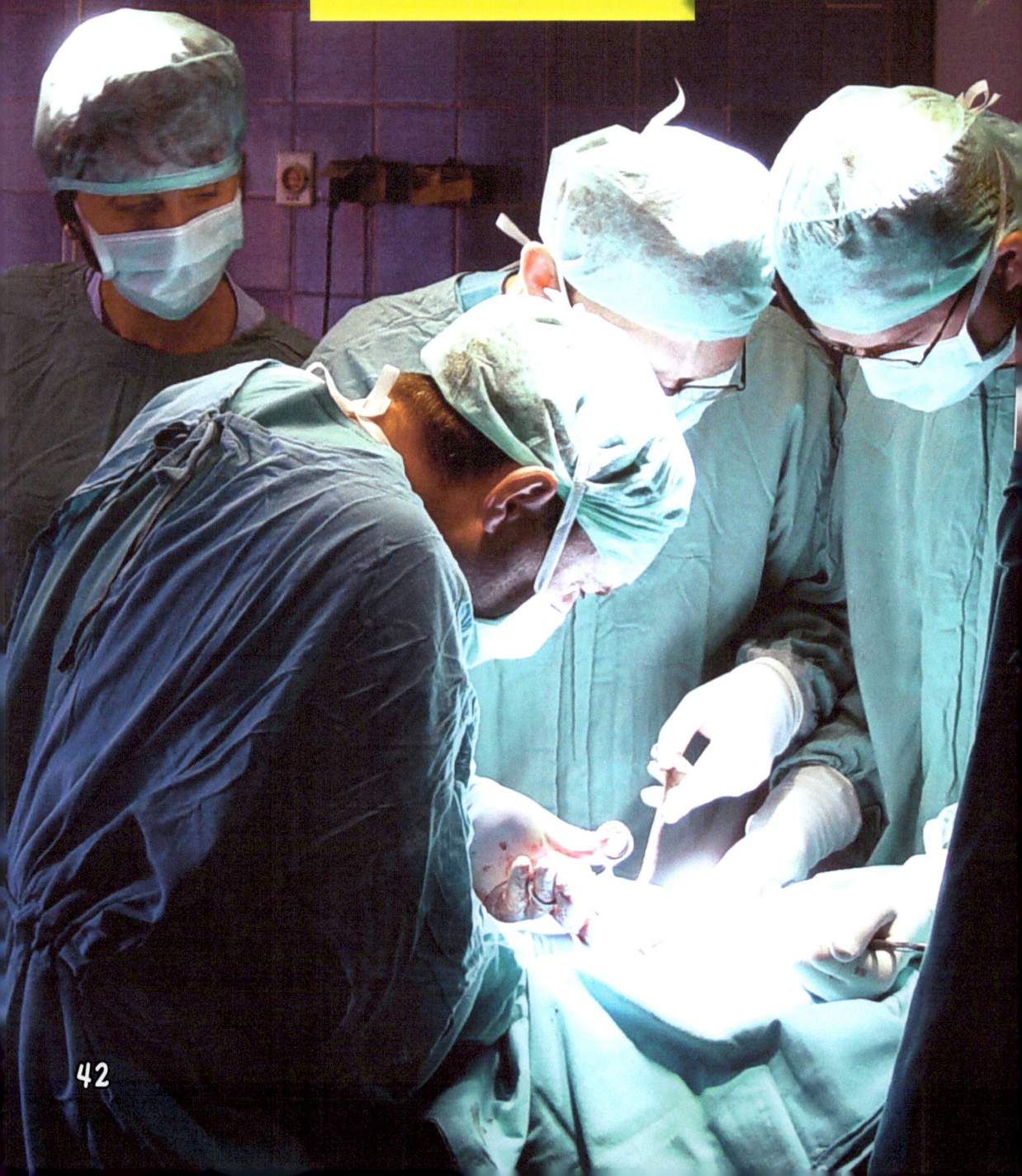

Surgery

Surgery is the oldest form of cancer treatment. It is also an important part of diagnosing cancer and finding out how far it has spread.

If you need to have a surgery, you will probably be admitted into a hospital. One of the workers in the hospital will take you to the operating room. Often, you will go there on a special bed with wheels. The room will have bright lights on the ceiling. While you are there, a special doctor called an *anesthesiologist* will give you medicine that makes you go to sleep. When you wake up, the surgery will be over.

Surgery is the best way to cure many types of cancer, especially those that have not spread to other parts of the body.

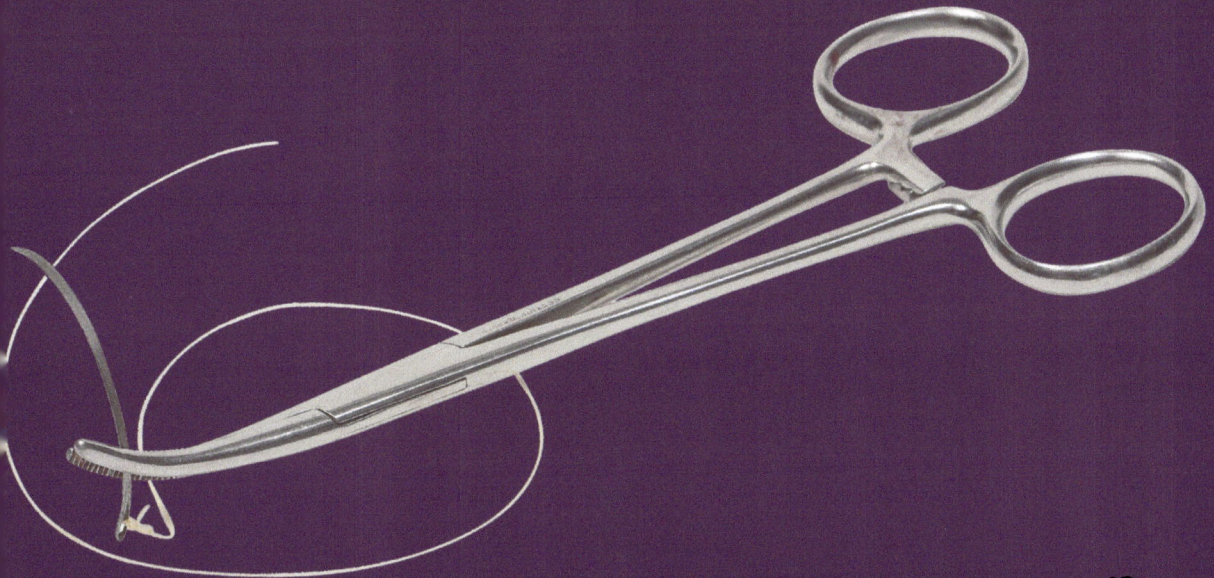

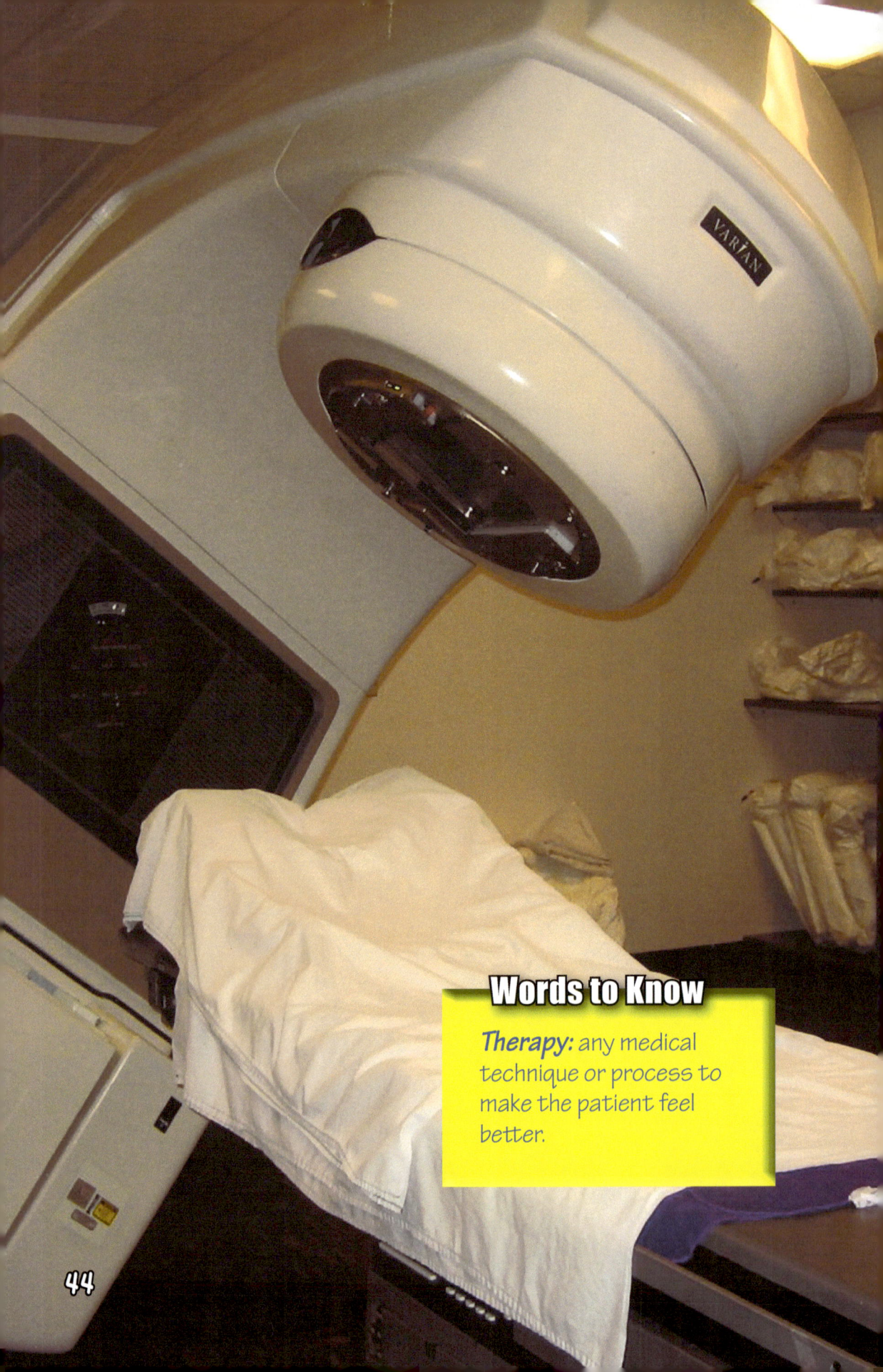

Words to Know

Therapy: any medical technique or process to make the patient feel better.

Radiation

If you have radiation *therapy*, you will lie on a bed like the ones shown on these pages. A machine will send radiation into your body. The radiation kills cancer cells. It also kills some normal cells, which is why radiation therapy may make your hair fall out. Don't worry—it will grow back!

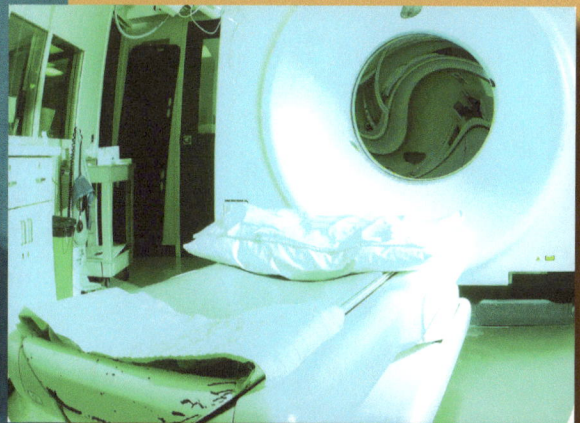

Chemotherapy

Chemotherapy—"chemo" for short—most often means you'll take certain medicines to treat your cancer. You might take these drugs before or after cancer surgery. You might take them along with radiation treatment. Or you might take the medicines alone. Your oncologist will decide what is the best treatment for the kind of cancer you have.

During chemotherapy, you may go into a hospital every week or every few weeks. While the medicine is being given to you (often through a tube that carries it into one of your blood vessels), you will sit in a chair, probably in a room that looks a little like the one on the page to the left.

Because the chemicals in the medicine affect both cancer cells and normal cells, chemotherapy often makes people feel sick. It is an important weapon in the battle against cancer, though. Because of it, many people with cancer will have full, healthy lives when their treatment is done.

Bone Marrow Transplants

When people have certain kinds of cancer, especially leukemia, cancer attacks their bone marrow. This can make them very sick. A bone marrow transplant takes bone marrow from a healthy person and puts it into a patient whose bone marrow is not working properly. This is one way to treat leukemia and other cancers.

Donated bone marrow must match the patient's tissue type. It is often taken from a close relative.

Bone marrow is taken from the *donor* in an operating room while the donor is asleep from anesthesia. Some of the donor's bone marrow is removed from the top of the hip bone. Then it will be put into the other person.

Alternative Treatments

Many people with cancer want to try treatments besides the ones we've mentioned here. These are sometimes called "alternative treatments." They include things like herbal medicines, meditation techniques, and traditional Asian medicines. Not all these treatments are safe, however. Many of them have very little effect on cancer. Doctors suggest that cancer patients use alternative cancer treatments along with treatments they receive from their doctors—but not instead of medical care. You should always tell your doctor if you use one of these treatments.

Alternative cancer treatments can help patients cope with pain and discomfort. They generally aren't strong enough to replace the medicines your doctor will give you. The following techniques may be helpful, though:

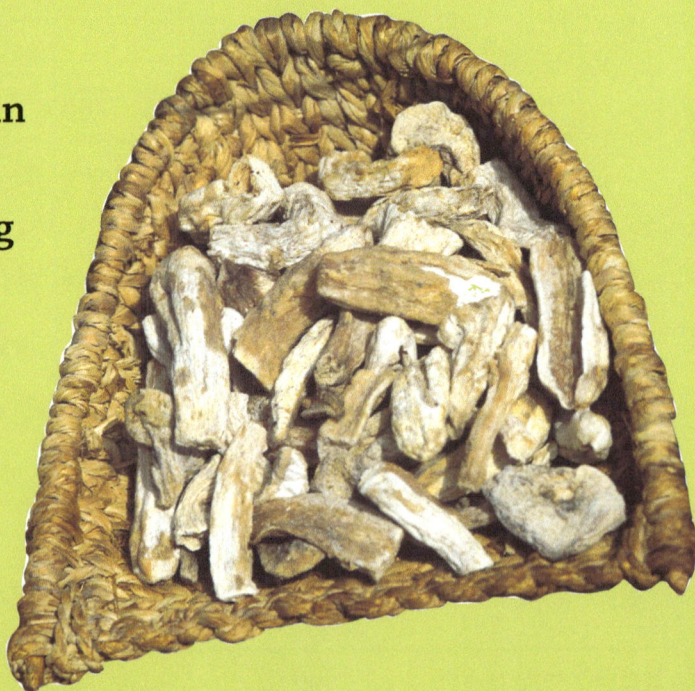

- *Yoga* can help sleep problems and improve energy levels during cancer treatment.
- *Acupuncture* can help you have less *nausea* and pain from chemotherapy.
- *Meditation* and prayer can help cancer patients cope with feeling sad and worried.

Words to Know

Yoga: a system of exercises to control the body and mind that is based on a Hindu religious practice.

Acupuncture: a Chinese medical practice in which specific body areas are pierced with fine needles to relieve pain.

Nausea: feeling like you're going to throw up.

Meditation: a deep state of awareness and relaxation.

Research

Did You Know?

In April 2008, the Russian Ministry of Public Health approved the world's first kidney cancer *vaccine*. The vaccine will help prevent kidney cancer from coming back once a patient has been successfully treated.

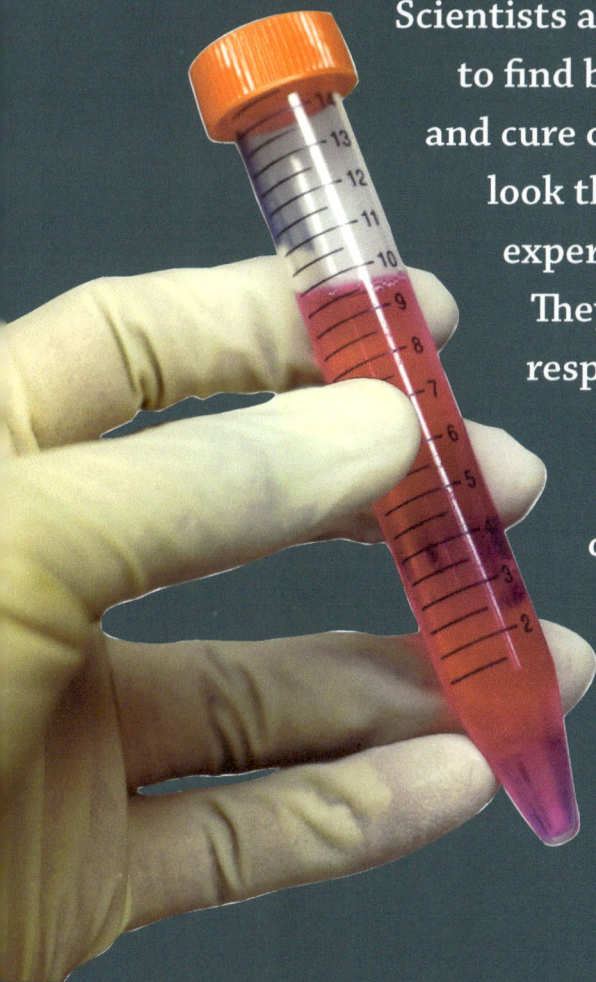

Scientists around the world are working to find better ways to prevent, treat, and cure cancer. They work in labs and look through microscopes. They do experiments on animals and cells. They carefully watch how people respond to different treatments. Their work is helping them better understand what causes cancer—and what can be done to both cure it and prevent it from happening. The more scientists understand about cancer, the more weapons doctors will have to fight it.

Words to Know

Vaccine: a substance that makes the immune system able to better fight off invaders, such as cancer cells or germs like bacteria and viruses. A vaccine is often given as a "shot."

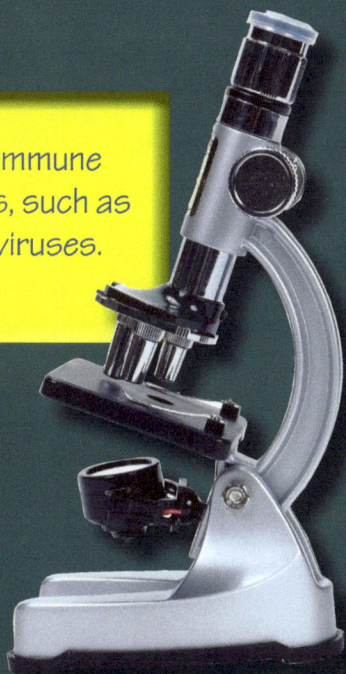

What the World is Doing to Find a Cure

Cancer affects everyone. Almost everyone in the world knows someone who has had this disease. That is why people around the world are becoming *activists* in the fight against cancer. Organizations like Livestrong, founded by cyclist Lance Armstrong who won his own battle against cancer, get people involved. They raise money for cancer research and promote awareness. *Marathons* and bike rides are one way to do this. Bracelets like the ones shown on this page also draw attention to breast cancer and other cancer causes.

According to the Livestrong website, when it comes to fighting cancer, unity is strength, knowledge is power, and attitude is everything!

Words to Know

Activists: people who take action to bring about some change in the world.

Marathons: long-distance races.

What You Can Do to Protect Yourself

Cancer is a scary disease—but you can take steps to protect yourself against it. One of the best ways to prevent cancer is to eat a healthy diet that includes plenty of fruits and vegetables. These foods contain chemicals that can actually help your body fight off cancer. You can also protect yourself by using sunscreen when you're out in the sun. And one of the best ways of all to fight cancer? Don't smoke!

Real Kids

Jamie Stafford's mom found out her son had leukemia when he was only eight months old. The entire family's life changed after that. Jamie had to be in the hospital for weeks at a time for treatment. Sometimes Jamie's treatments made him sick, too. He would come home, only to have a bad reaction to a medicine he was taking and have to go back in the hospital.

Did You Know?

Most children who have leukemia get better. They will often need chemotherapy and other treatments every year, however, to continue to be cancer-free.

Jamie's older sister Amanda also had a tough time through all this. She was worried about her baby brother. It made her sad to see him in the hospital.

She also felt lonely sometimes because her mother needed to spend so much time with Jamie. There wasn't much time left over for Amanda. Sometimes Amanda felt angry and jealous—and then she felt guilty. Amanda's feelings were perfectly normal, though, and she had nothing to feel guilty about.

Today, after three long years of treatment, Jamie is finally healthy again. Amanda's glad to have her baby brother back home for good.

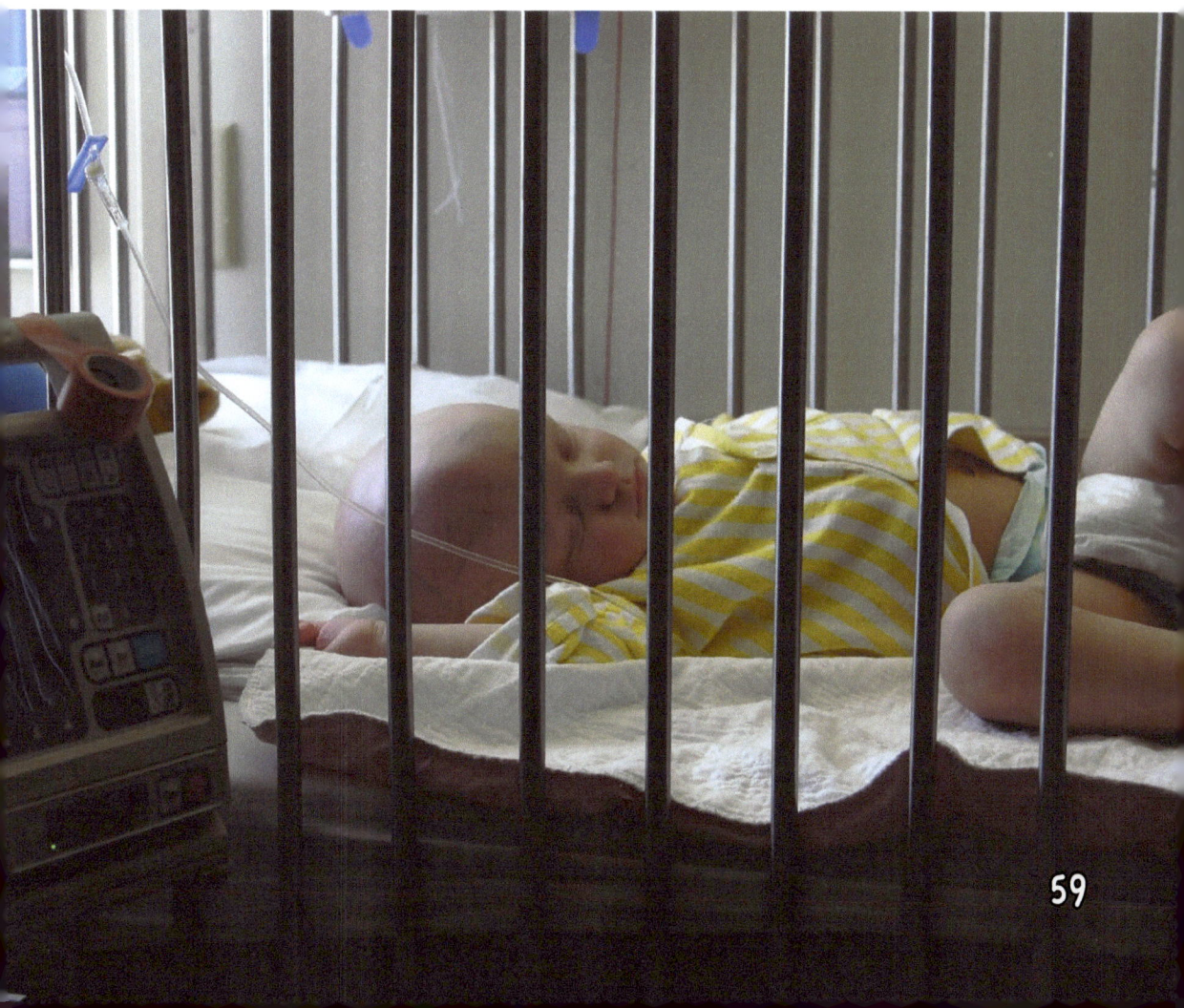

Find Out More

American Cancer Society
www.cancer.org

Cancer Resources
www.oncolink.org/index.cfm

Cancer Kids
www.cancerkids.org

Cancer Research UK
info.cancerresearchuk.org

Childhood Cancer
www.kidshealth.org/parent/medical/cancer/cancer.html

Children's Cancer Web
www.cancerindex.org/ccw/guide2y.htm

Mayo Clinic Cancer Awareness
www.mayoclinic.com/health/cancer/DS01076

National Cancer Institute
www.cancer.gov

World Health Organization/Cancer
www.who.int/cancer/en

Index

Picture Credits

About the Author

Rae Simons has written many books for young adults and children. She lives in upstate New York with her family.

About the Consultant

Elise DeVore Berlan, MD, MPH, FAAP, is a faculty member of the Division of Adolescent Health at Nationwide Children's Hospital and an Assistant Professor of Clinical Pediatrics at the Ohio State University College of Medicine. She completed her fellowship in adolescent medicine at Children's Hospital Boston and obtained a master's degree in public health at the Harvard School of Public Health. Dr. Berlan completed her residency in pediatrics at the Children's Hospital of Philadelphia, where she also served an additional year as chief resident. She received her medical degree from the University of Iowa College of Medicine.

www.ingramcontent.com/pod-product-compliance
Lightning Source LLC
Chambersburg PA
CBHW042017080426
42735CB00002B/82